KU-736-498

4

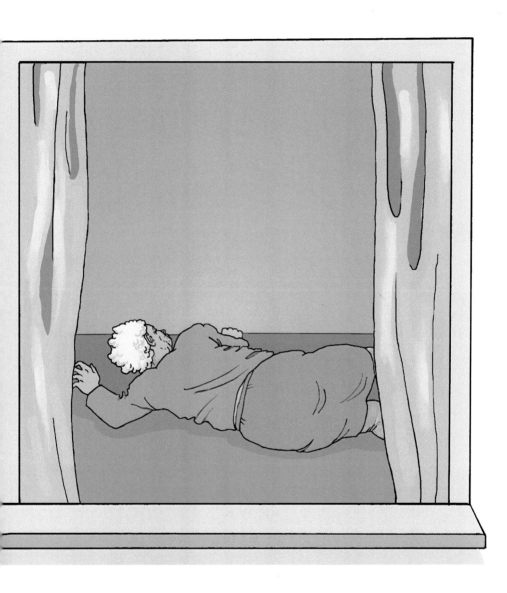

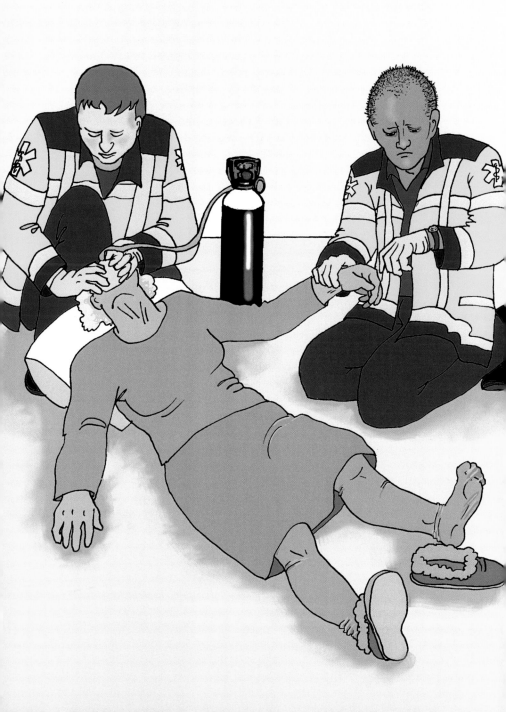

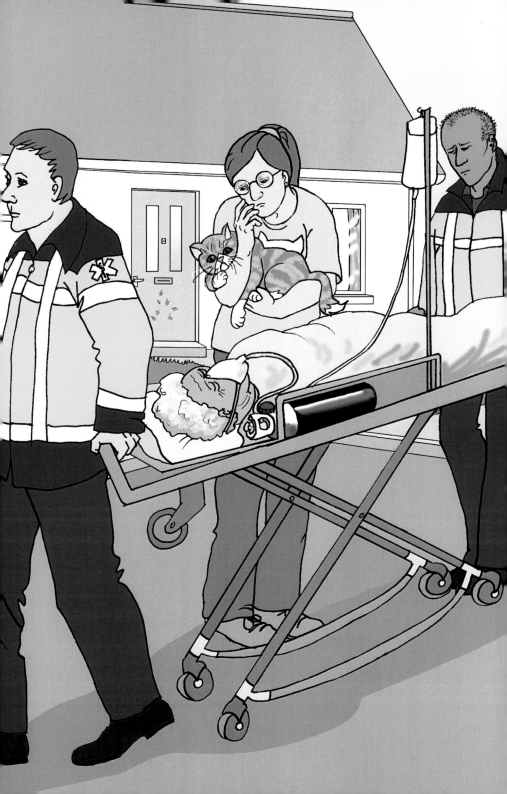

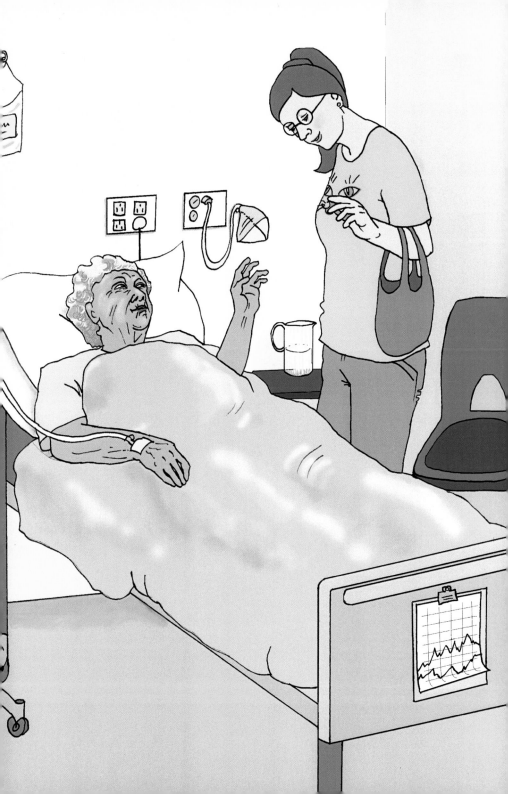

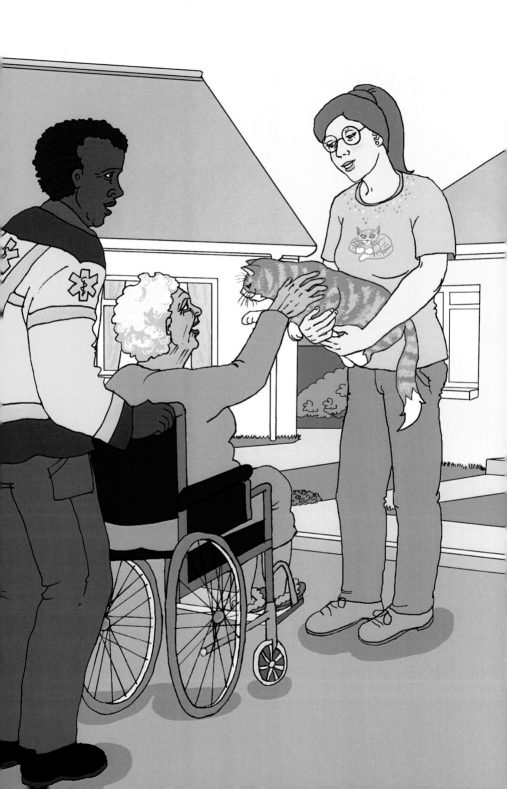

Storyline

The following words are provided for readers and supporters who want some ideas about one possible story. Most readers make their own story up from the pictures.

1. Mary loves cats.

2. Mrs Hill next door has a cat called Ginger.

3. Mary and Ginger are friends.

4. Mrs Hill gets cross when Mary talks to Ginger.

5. Mrs Hill takes Ginger inside. Mary and Ginger are very sad.

6. It starts to rain and Ginger wants to come in. Mary thinks Mrs Hill might get cross again.

7. It's late. Mary wonders why Mrs Hill hasn't let Ginger in for his tea.

8. Next morning, Ginger is still outside. He looks so sad. Mary thinks, "What's wrong?"

9. Mary gets dressed and goes next door.

10. She knocks, but there's no answer.

11. Mary and Ginger look in the window.

12. Oh dear! Mrs Hill is on the floor.

13. Mary and Ginger are scared!

14. Mary phones for help.

15. She tells the man on the phone about Mrs Hill.

16. A police officer comes.

17. So does a man with an ambulance.

18. The police officer opens the door with a special key.

19. The ambulance man and his friend help Mrs Hill.

20. They put Mrs Hill on a stretcher.

21. They put her in the ambulance.

22. Mary and Ginger worry about Mrs Hill.

23. Ginger is very hungry. Mary says, "I'll look after him."

24. The police officer gives Mary cat food for Ginger. They know Mrs Hill won't mind.

25. Mary picks up a photo of Ginger. "Can I borrow this, please?" she asks.

26. Mary feeds Ginger. He purrs. They both feel better.

27. Next day, Mary gets on a bus.

28. She gets off at the hospital.

29. She goes to see Mrs Hill.

30. She gives Mrs Hill the photo of Ginger. Mrs Hill is very pleased. She says, "Thank you for looking after him."

31. Next day, Mrs Hill comes home. She is very pleased to see Ginger, and Ginger is very happy to see her.

32. When Mrs Hill is better, she invites Mary to come to tea. She says, "Thank you for helping me." They are all friends now.

Beyond Words: Page Turners

Page Turners is a new series of short stories from Beyond Words for people who like to be inspired and entertained.

Each book in the Page Turners series is artist-written, and edited by the Beyond Words team and Series Editor Baroness Hollins. Our network of book clubs tell us what they think about the story and check out the pictures as we go along.

You can read Page Turners by yourself or with a reading group – you'll find there's plenty to talk about – and as with all Beyond Words books, the stories are just in pictures to make reading a pleasure.

Ginger is a Hero

Ginger is a Hero tells the story of Mary and the difficult relationship she has with her neighbour Mrs Hill. Mrs Hill keeps herself to herself and doesn't like it when Mary takes an interest in her cat, Ginger. But when Mary sees Ginger is locked out in the rain, she wonders why. Ginger leads Mary to Mrs Hill's window, and they discover the old lady collapsed on the floor. Ginger and Mary's quick thinking saves Mrs Hill's life.

Readers will find lots to enjoy and talk about in this gripping tale of how enemies become friends – all because of Ginger, the hero!

Bring your own artistic talents to Ginger and Mary's story. Download some of the pictures and colour them yourself here: www.booksbeyondwords.co.uk/bookshop/paperbacks/ginger-hero

Books Beyond Words

Books Beyond Words is our established range of stories for people who understand pictures better than words. The stories deal with things that can happen in anyone's life, and can help readers to talk about their own experiences, including some difficult or traumatic ones, or to learn about situations they may confront in their lives.

The books cover subject areas as diverse as health and lifestyle, bereavement, mental health, growing up, criminal justice and positive behaviour support.

A list of all Beyond Words publications, including print and eBook versions of Books Beyond Words titles, and where to buy them, can be found on our website:

www.booksbeyondwords.co.uk

Beyond Words training

Workshops for family carers, support workers and professionals about using Books Beyond Words are provided regularly in London, or can be arranged in other localities on request. Self-advocates are welcome. For information about forthcoming workshops see our website or contact us:

email: training@booksbeyondwords.co.uk
tel: 020 8725 5512

Video clips showing our books being read are also on our website and YouTube channel: www.youtube.com/user/booksbeyondwords and on our DVD, How to Use Books Beyond Words.

Related titles

The Drama Group (2015) by Hugh Grant, Sheila Hollins and Nigel Hollins, illustrated by Lisa Kopper. Dean goes to the theatre with his family. He enjoys it so much his friend James encourages him to go to a drama group. He's very nervous and finds it hard to join in at first. But once he gets to know people he has a really good time, doing both backstage roles and acting.

Falling in Love (1999) by Sheila Hollins, Wendy Perez and Adam Abdelnoor, illustrated by Beth Webb. This love story follows the relationship between Mike and Janet from their first date through to deciding to become engaged to be married.

George Gets Smart (2001) by Sheila Hollins, Margaret Flynn and Philippa Russell, illustrated by Catherine Brighton. George's life changes when he learns how to keep clean and smart. People no longer avoid being with him and he enjoys the company of his work mates and friends.

Enjoying Sport and Exercise (2008) by Sheila Hollins and Caroline Argent, illustrated by Catherine Brighton. *Enjoying Sport and Exercise* tells the story of three people who want to take up a sport and are supported to do so. Jasmine is a wheelchair user who takes up badminton while her mum does Tai Chi; Charlie, who is overweight, discovers dog walking and cricket; James is a runner who fulfils his ambition to run a marathon.

Author and illustrator

Beth Webb is the artist who helped to develop the very first Beyond Words books, linking emotionally-keyed colours with clear body language to enhance the simple illustrations. She is also a children's author and a professional storyteller.

Acknowledgments

With thanks to all our story triallers in Maidstone Book Club, St Joseph's Book Club, Hendon, Dover Discovery Book Club, Dartford Library Book Club, Bromley Sparks: Gillian Rees, Teresa Durman, and Nigel Hollins; Ann, Edward, Eric, Jonathan, Kevin, Nicky and Sammy from the Tunbridge Wells Book Worms.

Additional thanks to Chloë and Mary for their invaluable help, and special thanks to Izzy (who posed for Ginger).

How to read this book

There is no right or wrong way to read this book. Remember it is not necessary to be able to read the words.

1. Some people are not used to reading books. Start at the beginning and read the story in each picture. Encourage the reader to hold the book themselves and to turn the pages at their own pace.

2. Whether you are reading the book with one person or with a group, encourage them to tell the story in their own words. You may think something different is happening in the pictures yourself, but that doesn't matter. Don't challenge the reader(s) or suggest their ideas are wrong.

3. You can help readers along by asking questions like:

- Who do you think that is?
- What is happening?
- How is he or she feeling?
- Do you ever feel like that?

4. You don't have to read the whole book in one sitting. Have fun with it: allow people time to chat about what they are reading and to follow the pictures at their own pace.